ON OPPOSITE

SIDES

OF THE DOOR

ON OPPOSITE

SIDES

OF THE DOOR

Debbora Hanna

www.AnointedFireHouse.com

On Opposite Sides of the Door
Copyright © 2015
Author: Debbora Hanna
Email: info@anointedfire.com

Cover design: Anointed Fire™ House
Publisher: Anointed Fire™ House
Publisher's Website: www.anointedfirehouse.com

ISBN-10: 978-0692575451

ISBN-13: 0692575456

Special thanks to my husband, Heyward Hanna. Without you being my support and my friend, none of this would have been possible.

I would like to dedicate this book to my children: Kimberly, Russell and Dwayne because they were my motivation for success.

Acknowledgments

- I have watched Brenda struggle over the years, since her recovery from addiction, to become the woman she is today. I am so proud of who she has become. She has really grown to be a remarkable woman of God and an awesome praise and worship leader.

- My connection with Faith was divinely orchestrated by God. Her passion to reach out to hurting women is intrinsically connected to her life's story; and her struggle to overcome her own addiction. Faith is a woman of faith, love and compassion, I am honored to call her my friend.

- Helen is a survivor. She had come from a place of giving up on life and ready to die from cancer, to having to piece her life back together, because God is not finished with her. Where others counted her out, God gave her a second chance at life. Helen is now in the process of becoming who God created her to be.

Table of Contents

Introduction

On Opposite Sides of The Door is a
story of three women whose lives led them
down a path that could have easily landed
them on the opposite side of the prison doors
for good, but their lives took a turn for the
better.

**"Although we had the keys, we could not
open the door."**

DEBBORA'S STORY

In my family, I was the person everyone turned to in troubled times. Some even compared me to "Big Momma" from the movie *Soul Food* because I was always trying to keep the family together by providing emotional and financial support when needed, plus, I was responsible for organizing family gatherings.

Sometimes, I gave to others without them having to ask, because I knew that they were in need. It wasn't long before I began to notice that the only time I would receive a call from anyone was when they wanted me to bail them out of a bad situation. I was always giving, but never getting anything in return.

My story began in 1961. I was the sixth of seven children and I turned out to be more business-minded than my other siblings. My oldest brother went off to join the Marine Corp and he never returned to Baltimore, Maryland to live.

My mother was not raised by her mother because her father was very abusive. She and her siblings were raised by her uncle, a World War II veteran. This same uncle had come back from war "shell shocked", or better yet, what they now refer to as "Post Traumatic Stress Syndrome." He also sold one of my mother's sisters (Aunt Viola) to his sister in Virginia for a bottle of wine.

My mother quit school in the sixth grade to work and take care of my Aunt Lucille and make sure she finished school. She said that her only desire was to find a good man who would take care of her. When she married my father, she thought she'd found that man, but she soon learned that he did not love her the way she loved him. In fact, he said later that he did not love her at all. One day, my father came home from work and left a note on the table telling my mother to "get on welfare." He left her to raise six children alone. This devastated my mother because she always told us that she "worshipped the ground my father walked on."

I was very young when my father left and I hadn't started school yet, so the only memory I have of him is a memory of him disciplining me for eating some peanut butter when I was supposed to be in bed. I remember him making me sit at the kitchen table and eat half a jar of peanut butter.

After my parents separated, my mother had another baby. She then had to raise seven children alone while on welfare.

I respected my mother for not doing to us what her mother did to her and her siblings. I understand now that she did what she thought she had to do in order to survive, but I still did not want to be like her. I remember how my mother struggled to raise her children while relying on welfare. We went hungry a lot of the time because the food stamps did not last the entire month.

The money she received was barely enough to pay the rent, utilities and buy some of the personal things we needed. However, during that time (the 1960's), the government wasn't giving families as much as they do now, so we went without the basic necessities many times because she simply could not afford them. Since our housing options were limited to my mother's income, we lived in poor neighborhoods.

We were living on McDonough Street and I was on my way to my best friend Mary's house when I was taken at gunpoint by two neighborhood boys. I knew one of the boys, but I didn't know the other one. They took me to the aunt's house of the boy I didn't know and raped me. I was only eleven years old at the time. After the attack was over, they told me to leave. I left there confused and wondering why they did what they did to me. Feeling ashamed, I went home, took a bath and stayed in the house for the remainder of the day. I didn't tell my mother or anyone, for that matter, because they threatened to kill me if I told anyone.

That incident took a huge toll on my life, both emotionally and socially.

When I turned twelve, I began to experiment with alcohol and marijuana. I'm sure that the rape factored into my choice to lead such a reckless life. I could have chosen a different path, but I didn't. Even though I made mistakes and bad decisions, I was always determined not to end up like my mother.

You can choose to become a victim of your environment or a victor because of it. I became a victor.

In 1974, we moved to Perlman Place because of our limited housing options. Perlman Place was a narrow street between North Avenue and Sinclair Lane. It was there that my youngest sister, Kimberly, was killed at the age of five. She was outside playing and I was on my way to visit one of my friends. She asked me if she could go with me, but I told her no. My brother, Charles, was across the street from our house; he was in the school yard playing baseball, and Kimberly went to the school yard to be with him. Charles brought her back across the street to the house, and as soon as he went back to the school yard, she went between two parked cars. She was trying to cross the street again, but when she stepped from between the cars, another car came along and hit her. To make matters worse, the driver dragged my sister for half a block down the street before realizing that she had hit her. Needless to say, I felt responsible for my sister's death because I did not take her with me.

I can only imagine how my brother, Charles, felt. I believe it may have affected him more because he was the one who picked Kim up and ran ten blocks to Johns Hopkins Hospital with her in his arms. When I heard the news, I ran to the hospital, but by the time I arrived, she had already expired and I was not allowed to see her. I was devastated. My friend and little sister was gone, and I never got the chance to apologize or to tell her that I loved her.

Moving on from there was not easy because there were many times when I would close my eyes and see Kim standing in front of me. I had many sleepless nights because we shared the same room, and all of a sudden, I was sleeping alone. I don't remember if anyone offered me grief counseling, but I never received counseling, so I dealt with Kim's death the best way I could. Eventually, I learned to adjust to my new life and I learned to cope. Looking back, I believe that children should receive counseling when they lose a sibling because we don't know how they cope with death or how it will affect them in the future.

From time to time, I still wonder what she would look like today or how she would have turned out if she had the opportunity to grow up.

Just telling this story has stirred up some emotions that I thought I had gotten over.

Two years after the death of Kim, I got pregnant by a thirty-one year old man. I was only fourteen years old. I struggled with the thought of having an abortion, but my mother, being a religious woman, would not hear of it, plus, my sister, Brenda, was also pregnant. We agreed that if we were having girls, whoever had her baby first could name the baby Kimberly.

I had my baby five days before Brenda had her daughter. I named her Kimberly. I believe that God allowed me to be first so I could cope better. I also believe that if Brenda had named her daughter Kimberly, I would still be ridden with guilt. For me, this was my way of keeping Kimberly alive. Not only did I get to name my daughter after my sister, but I got to raise her as well.

Being that I was a teenage mother, my mother knew that I was not ready for that kind of responsibility. So, for the first two years of my daughter's life, my mother took care of her so I could focus on finishing school. I believe that she helped me a lot because she missed her Kimberly as well, so we both played a part in raising my daughter. My mother was a tremendous help to me until I got pregnant with my second child at the age of seventeen. I had my second child by a thirty-six year old man (Russell), whom

I later married. After my second pregnancy, my mother told me that it was time for me to take responsibility and raise my own children, so I moved in with Russell.

At the age of nineteen, I had my third child and I named him Dwayne. After Dwayne was born, Russell and I got married.

While we were dating, I was infatuated with Russell, and of course, I thought it was love, but again, I was only seventeen and did not really know what love was. If Russell hadn't been so jealous, I probably could have fallen in love with him, but his jealousy killed whatever chance there was of that ever happening.

Needless to say, because he was extremely jealous, my husband became verbally and physically abusive. That should not have been a surprise to me because when we were dating, I saw his violent side. I was at a little hole in the wall bar with some girlfriends and decided to step outside to get some fresh air. While I was standing outside, a gentleman I knew walked up and was about to enter the bar. When he saw me, he stayed outside and talked with me. While we were talking, Russell pulled up and saw us there. He jumped out of his car, ran up to the man and started beating him with his fist. While he was punching him, he said, "You took my wife, and now, you're trying to take my girlfriend."

That should have been a red flag, but at that time, I did not know the whole story behind the breakup of his marriage. The only thing I knew was that Russel's ex-wife had mental health issues and the man I had been speaking with was romantically involved with her, so it appeared that his anger was towards the man and not me.

Ladies no matter how much we want to, we can't change a man.
When you see the warning signs, believe them and run like crazy!

After I moved in with Russell, he didn't want me to have any friends or go to work outside of the home. When my family came to visit, he always found a reason to argue in front of them, so it was obvious that he had a problem with them visiting me. He wanted me to stay at home and totally depend on him for financial support. I needed emotional support from him, but I did not receive it. Even though he didn't make a lot of money and we struggled financially, he wanted to control me so I was not allowed to work.

Whenever I needed something, I had to ask him. I had to even ask him for money to buy my personals and this was very embarrassing because I had to explain why I needed them. *(This was very frustrating for me because he acted more like a strict father than a husband.)* Every weekend, we would argue and fight over any and everything, mainly because of his jealousy and insecurities. I believe he didn't trust me because I was so much younger than him. Russell worked every day and paid the bills, but he was a functional alcoholic. He drank a six pack of beer and a fifth of liquor every night, and since he was the manager of a liquor store, he would bring his drinks home every night. His first wife had cheated on him, so he believed that women were incapable of being faithful. He didn't give me the chance to be the kind of wife I could have been, so every night he would get drunk, play cheating songs on the record player and accused me of cheating. This always led to a physical fight. The twisted images he conjured up in his mind about what I was doing while he was at work made my life miserable. Of course, after years of being accused of cheating, I finally did.

Do I think my affair was justified? No. An affair is never justified because it always hurts the one who has been cheated on. Was I remorseful? No, because by then, the relationship was over for me emotionally and physically. Something as small as watching him chew his food made me sick to my stomach. Unfortunately, I had grown to despise him.

One night, during an argument, Russell threatened to kill me, and when he grabbed his shotgun, I got my six-month-old son (Dwayne) out of his crib and ran downstairs. While I was trying to open the front door, he pointed the gun at us and said, "I hope to God there is a bullet in here," and he pulled the trigger. I thank God there were no bullets in the gun or my baby and I would not be here today.

Fear turned into anger and I laid Dwayne on the floor, grabbed the machete that was hanging on the wall and ran up the stairs after him. I grabbed him by the throat and put the blade up to his neck. I heard a voice say, "Push it and watch his head roll down the stairs." The only reason I did not go through with it was because Kimberly and Russell Jr. came out of their room and when they saw what was happening, they started crying. I looked at my babies and realized that I could not kill their father in front of them, but he had no problem with attempting to kill me with my baby in my arms.

This encounter was just one of many violent encounters we had over the course of our relationship. Our house had turned into a war zone because of our volatile marriage.

The only communication we had was when he was home yelling, arguing and accusing me of cheating. I started to believe that he wasn't happy unless there was tension in our home. When he was at work, the house would be peaceful and we were happy, but as soon as he walked into the house, the whole atmosphere changed. The children were always sent to their rooms and he would begin with his interrogation. Russell wanted total control of everything regarding me, so in 1982, he put call forwarding on our house phone. I did not know anything about call forwarding at that time. He would forward our calls to his job's number when he went to work, because he was trying to monitor who was calling me while he was at work. It had not occurred to me that the phone didn't ring while he was at work; it would only ring when he was at home. When I realized what was happening, I confronted him and he admitted to transferring the calls. Needless to say, the arguing started again. I went to the bedroom because I was tired of arguing with him and he did what he did best; he drank his beers and his fifth of liquor, pulled out his handgun, played cheating songs, sat on the sofa and fell asleep with the gun lying beside him. Russell Jr., who was only four years old at the time, brought the gun into my bedroom and said, "Mommy, look what I've got."

When I saw him with the gun, knowing that it was loaded, I calmly said to him, "Sweetie, give me the gun." He handed it to me and I put it under the mattress where I was sitting on my bed. When my husband woke up, he came into the bedroom looking for the gun and I told him what had happened. I told him that I had the gun. You would think that a forty year old man would know better than to leave a loaded gun lying around where children could get to it, but we are not talking about someone who was a rational thinker.

He wanted me to give the gun to him, and when I refused, he tried to pull me off the bed so he could get it himself. I was terrified, but I refused to let him take it. I guess you can say it was a combination of adrenaline and him being drunk, but when he tried to move me off the bed to retrieve the gun, I managed to pick him up and toss him over my head to the other side of the bedroom.

He got back up, came around to where I was standing and tried again to take the gun. Somehow, I managed to throw him on the floor, hold him down with one hand and dial 911 with the other hand.

When the police arrived, they did not press charges. Instead, they took the handguns out of the house and told him that after they ran a check on them, he could come to the station to get them. They said this process would take about seven days. When Russell went to the police station to get his guns back, he was unable to do so because they had put the guns in my name. Needless to say, I was not going to get them, so the only guns left in the house were his shotguns. That was no real consolation, because I could be shot with those as well.

I think that the reason I stayed with him as long as I did was because I did not see myself as a victim of domestic violence, or maybe I did not know enough about domestic violence to know that I was a victim because I fought back. The women I was around never used the term domestic violence, even though I was not the only one in the group who had to fight in her relationship. People made you believe that this was just a part of relationships.

At that time, I did not realize just how sick and twisted his behavior was; it was just something I dealt with. It could have been that there was something sick and twisted about my thinking as well. I had never sought counseling to see what the root of that problem was, but the truth is we sometimes choose security over stability. Could it be that women in abusive relationships believe that because their partners take care of them and provides a secure place for them to stay that they should put up with the abuse? Many women in abusive relationships believe that just because their lovers cry or say they're sorry that things would change, but there are some deep rooted anger issues that need to be addressed before a change happens. Ladies, you can't love him or mother him out of his issues, so if you are in an abusive relationship or if you are the abuser, **PLEASE GET HELP BEFORE IT ENDS TRAGICALLY!** Now that I know what domestic violence is, I will no longer allow myself to be its victim.

Was I afraid to leave? Yes. For me, thinking about trying to raise three children alone with no job was scary enough. Not wanting to follow in my mother's footsteps was also a scary option, but I knew that if I did not leave, his death or my death was inevitable. I had even devised a plan to kill him.

It was 1983 when I heard an announcement on the radio about cyanide poisoning being found in certain wine bottles, so I got some cyanide to put in his liquor. I actually thought it was a good plan and I probably would have gotten away with it, but I thank God for a praying mother. At this point, I was so tired that I kept telling myself that the relationship had to end, not even considering the consequences. I believe had she not been praying, I would have acted on my frustrations.

After eight years of dealing with emotional and physical abuse, I finally mustered up the courage to leave him. I remember that day like it was yesterday. After Russell had gone to work, I went to my children's school to have them transferred out. I then came home to pack my things, and while I was packing, Russell walked in the front door. He came home early from work because he had taken ill. Fear gripped me and I thought I was not going to get out alive, but when he went to the bedroom, the cab pulled up. I grabbed whatever bags I could carry, ran out the front door, jumped into the cab and told the driver to hurry up and pull off.

My three children and I went to live with my oldest sister and her three children in their two bedroom apartment. It was a little crowded, but I was just grateful for a peaceful place to live and a sister who was willing to help. If I didn't have a praying mother and the support of my oldest sister, I believe I would have either been dead or serving a life sentence in prison for murder.

Even after I left him and moved on with my life, Russell still did vicious things to try and hurt me without any consideration of how his actions would affect the children. **But when you are a selfish individual, the only one who matters to you is you.**

Based on some events that had taken place in my life, I believe that one of Satan's assignments was to try to get me on the other side of the prison door, but God had another plan for my life.

John 10:10 Authorized (King James) Version (AKJV)

"The thief cometh not, but for to steal, and to kill, and to destroy: I am come that they might have life, and that they might have it more abundantly."

After that tumultuous relationship, I purposed that I would never depend on another man, nor would I rely on the welfare system for support.

Watching my mother struggle to raise us affected me emotionally, but not in a negative way. It made me angry enough to want to change my circumstances. I've heard people say that they were poor but did not know that they were poor because being poor was all they knew. Well, I was poor and

I knew that I was poor. I did not like what poverty looked or felt like. At that time, however, I did not know what I wanted, but I knew what I did not want, and that was to continue to struggle. Because I refused to raise my children on welfare, I took back the power that I had given my abusive spouse, and in 1987, I finished college with my Associates degree in Health Information Technology. I started working at one of The Johns Hopkins Health Plans, but I was unable to make a decent living for myself and my children with my wages of only $5.25 an hour.

After working there for a year, I took the correctional officer's test and passed. I was hired on September 21, 1988. This provided me with the salary I needed to be totally independent of any social service programs.

I was assigned to the Maryland State Penitentiary, a maximum security prison. In 1989, I was assigned to work the segregation unit (lock-up) when I was attacked and stabbed by an inmate. Every time I was assigned to work that unit, the sergeant would assign me to work the third tier. This was the tier that had a hole in the floor. They had put wood boards over the hole to create a walkway. I was also told that the third tier was where they put the smaller officers because they could walk over the boards without falling through them.

On this particular morning, the shift captain told the senior officers in roll call to inform the junior officers they were working with about the problem inmates on their unit. This did not happen for me and the sergeant who was assigned to the property room came to my tier to pack an inmate up and move him over to the new super maximum security prison on Madison Street.

It was a known fact that this particular inmate was combative with officers because he did not want to go into the general population. He owed money to some inmates in population and was afraid to come out of segregation, so he would intentionally assault staff so he could stay in segregation. Unfortunately, I was not informed of this until it was too late.

The proper protocol had not been followed. There were supposed to be two officers to break a segregation inmate out of his cell, but the sergeant took a shortcut and let the inmate out himself. While the sergeant was in the inmate's cell inventorying his property, I was on my way off the tier to get my count sheet. When the inmate saw me, he ran down the tier and jumped me from behind. He stabbed me five times before the sergeant realized what was happening.

Had it not been for the inmate tier man telling the sergeant what was happening, I don't know how long it would have taken for him to come out of the cell and assist me.

When the sergeant finally came out of the cell and got the inmate off of me, I was able to use my two-way radio and call for assistance.

Once the response team arrived, I was taken to the institutional hospital and they determined that I needed sutures. I was taken to Johns Hopkins Hospital where I was treated and released. After being off work for a month, I decided to go back because I knew the risks involved when I took the job. I was very much aware that I was working with inmates who were serving long-term sentences for some very serious crimes.

I was still thinking about providing a better life for my children, so I came back to work and I told my lieutenant to put me in the yard because I wanted to let the inmates know that they did not defeat me. I experienced firsthand that there was no guarantee that I would walk out that prison door and not be carried out in a body bag. After that incident, I decided that I would not tolerate officers who compromised or took "shortcuts" because my life was at stake. That meant I had to write up officers who were not doing their jobs and this made me the enemy of many officers. My daughter later told me she was afraid that I was going to die. I was determined to be a person of integrity because I wanted to go home safely every day to my family and I knew that the other officers wanted the same thing.

Again I thank God for a praying mother. If nothing else, my mother prayed and I know that's what had gotten us through many tough times.

James 5:16: *"Confess your faults one to another, and pray one for another, that ye may be healed. The effectual fervent prayer of a righteous man availeth much."*

After being on the job for three years, my financial status improved and I was able to take my children out of the rental property we were living in. I bought my first house, a car and had money in my savings account. I felt obligated to help my family, and that's when their demand outweighed my supply. I sacrificed so much for others to the point that I started drowning in debt. I was maxing out my credit cards to help them pay their bills, buy food and clothes for their children and buy furniture for their houses. I don't blame them because I tried to come to everybody's rescue. (You can't help people who don't want to help themselves and you can't change people who don't want to change.)

I thought the reason they were content with where they were was because they were not motivated or encouraged to do better. I had been motivated by watching my mother struggle all those years and the fact that my siblings and I didn't have the things other children had. I didn't want my children to feel a sense of hopelessness. Sometimes, I worked two jobs to make sure they did not go without the things they wanted and needed because I could not depend on their fathers for child support. Unfortunately, the courts determined that my ex-husband only had to pay $140 a month for our two children and my daughter's father was only paying $48 a month. Bi-weekly groceries cost more than what they were giving, and that's not to mention that I had to buy clothes for them too. I made up my mind to never beg my children's fathers to do for their children what they should have done without prompting, nor was I going to become bitter or resentful towards them. I did not speak ill of my children's fathers to them because they were traumatized enough and I did not want to become a negative influence in their lives. Unfortunately, Russell Sr. did not share the same sentiment. He had no problem trying to portray me as a villain every time the boys were with him. It didn't matter to him that he was further destroying the way his sons related to women. Russell Jr. was affected by his father's poison because in his mind, his father could do no wrong, but Dwayne was determined to not be like his father.

Although Russell Sr. is deceased and Russell Jr. is now thirty-six years old, I only pray that he will break free of his father's negative influence because he now has three sons of his own. I didn't want him to do to his sons what his father did to him, but unfortunately, history does repeat itself.

Why is it that some men feel that when their marriages or relationships are over, they have to be done with the children as well and all of their responsibility stops? Note: **Guys, hear me out: When you divorce the mother of your children, don't divorce the children because they really need you emotionally and financially.**

It is important for us to become educated about finances because for too long, many of us have accepted poverty as being a part of life. If nothing else, we need to make sure that in the event of our deaths, our children are well taken care of. I understand that when you are struggling financially, life insurance is the last thing on your mind.

After all, the first bill people usually let go of is life insurance. I know this because I used to be an insurance agent. In 1996, when my oldest sister (Susan) died from breast cancer, my father, oldest brother and I were the ones who paid for her funeral arrangements because she had no insurance. I was tasked with making the funeral arrangements, writing the obituary and picking out her clothes while trying to keep her three children from falling apart. Two months later, my grandmother passed and we were called upon again to help pay for arrangements because she had no insurance.

At that point, I was very angry because people who live for the day are inconsiderate of others. How could you not have life insurance? How could you think that once you're gone that life ends for everyone else?

Please don't leave your loved ones to have to worry about how you are going to be buried. It is hard enough to lose someone you love, but to have to ask people to help you bury your loved one while you are trying to grieve, can cause you to resent the one who is deceased for putting your family in this situation.

I did not realize just how much anger I was harboring until I had taken a grievance class at my church. At that time, I was dating Heyward. He was an officer as well. We met at the Maryland State Penitentiary in 1988, began dating in 1995 and married 1999. Heyward was there for me through the death of my sister and my grandmother, and he was a big support for me emotionally. He even assisted me in writing Susan's obituary. He understood how stressful it was for me to be outwardly strong for everybody else while falling apart on the inside because of the entire burden that had been placed on me. Being able to be transparent about my feelings without being made to feel like I was wrong or that I should feel bad about how I felt was such a relief. With Heyward, I was able to express how I really felt. I waited four years before I married Heyward because I did not want to bring another man to live in my house with my children. By the time we married, my youngest son, Dwayne, was in his last year of high school and Kimberly and Russell had already left home. As of today, Heyward and I have been together for twenty years and married for sixteen years. I believe that God gave me the man I needed, not the man I wanted. He has definitely been the glue in our relationship. Heyward's mother suffered with mental illness. She was diagnosed with Schizophrenia and I believe that her condition is the reason he was more tolerant and understanding of my emotional highs and lows.

Even after we were married, I still tried to rescue others, all the while, hiding from him how I was spending my money. It began to weigh heavy on our relationship because he felt that I was being secretive. Trying to help family almost destroyed not just me, but our relationship as well, because as much as I wanted to help others, I could no longer afford to. I took all of my frustrations out on him because I felt he did not understand my need to help, so my attitude towards him, at that time, was very unpleasant. I said everything to him that I wanted to say to others but didn't.

One night, in 2002, I was so angry with my husband that I started taking his clothes out of the closet and I tried to make him leave. If anyone had asked me why I was so angry with him, I wouldn't have had an answer. There was a physical altercation, I called the police and I was the one arrested that night because he had bruises on him, but I did not. I couldn't believe that I was being arrested. The entire time I was in the back of the police cruiser, I was in disbelief, wondering what had just happened. After all, I called them!

Heyward called my daughter, Kim, and told her about the incident. He asked her to pick me up from Central Booking when I was released, and he went to his brother's house that night.

When I arrived at the Central Booking and Intake Facility (CBIF), the arresting officer told the booking officer that I was a correctional officer. They fingerprinted and photographed me, but they did not put me in a cell. The officers allowed me to sit at the officer's station until I was able to see the Court Commissioner. I was processed quickly and released on my own recognizance because I had no prior record. That was nothing but the favor of God because during the ride to CBIF, the officer said that he was supposed to pick up another female, but he took me straight to the facility in the cruiser alone.

This is another instance where Satan tried to put and keep me on the opposite side of the door, but God had another plan because this incident could have cost me my job. After all, we had a Domestic Violence policy and I violated that policy. *Not only was I an officer working in the prison system, but I was also a professing Christian who was trying to live the Christian life.*

Being a Christian does not mean that you are perfect; we all mess up, but when God has a plan for your life and you trust Him, He will always guide you to the path you need to take, regardless of how unpleasant it is.

One year before this incident, God spoke to me while I was in prayer and said, "No matter what you go through, don't leave your husband."

After I was released from Central Booking, I came home to an empty apartment because Heyward was at his brother's house. I thought very long and hard about whether or not I should call him because I was angry and hurt. God began to speak to me, and He told me to call him and work on my marriage. I swallowed my pride, called him and he agreed to come home. When he came home, we talked, cried and prayed together. We agreed that we were going to work on our marriage.

(Heyward always said that he did not get married to get divorced, and he stayed true to that, fighting to make the marriage work, even when I wanted to give up.)

Although we had agreed to work on our marriage, I was still hurt and confused. After Heyward went to bed, I stayed up to talk to God. While I was praying and asking God why I was the one arrested, He said that if He had allowed Heyward to get arrested, the marriage would have been over. God said to me that the reason I had to get arrested was to save my marriage and to humble me.

I thank God because I don't have a record behind this incident and we did not separate either. As a matter of fact, my arrest made our relationship stronger. I did not realize it at the time, but God was using my husband to teach me how to deal with my issues and not run from them. I still didn't

42

understand the magnitude of what God had in store for me, but it all became clear to me in 2004 when my sister was arrested.

Our trials are not to turn us away from God, but to draw us closer to Him.

It doesn't matter what's going on in your life or how you think you have failed God , when He has a plan for your life, He will still order your steps and get you to where you need to be when you need to be there.

Psalm 37:23 Authorized (King James) Version (AKJV)

"The steps of a good man are ordered by the LORD: and he delighteth in his way."

My desire to help others played a huge part in some of the problems Heyward and I had. I didn't want to talk about my finances with him. On many occasions, he tried to talk to me about my finances, but for peace's sake, he stopped pushing the issue. When I could no longer help my family, the calls stopped and I had no one I could turn to for help.

Finally, I began to take Heyward's feelings into consideration and to think about how important my marriage was to me. Heyward was the one I could turn to when I needed money, but I was giving mine away to people who didn't plan to pay me back, nor did they appreciate all that I sacrificed for them. So, as difficult as it was, I had to start saying that I didn't have it to give. Those words became my favorite weapons because they caused all of those who were just using me to stay away.

After years of struggling to get back on my feet and pay down my debt, I learned to choose *who* to help and *when* to help. This lesson proved to be very valuable in 2004.

In 2003, I was promoted to sergeant and transferred to The Division of Pre-Trial Detention and Services. In 2004, while working at the Women's Detention Center in the Baltimore City Jail. I was assigned to the evening shift when my sister, Brenda, was arrested. This was one of those times where it was the *when* and *who* to help.

God knew when it was my time to get promoted. He orchestrated my life and ordered my steps so that I could be right where I needed to be when I needed to be there, because He knew when Brenda was coming there. Although you may not understand now, just know that God is making your crooked path straight. When you don't see a way, He is making a way out of no way.

Isaiah 45:2 Authorized (King James) Version (AKJV)

"I will go before thee, and make the crooked places straight: I will break in pieces the gates of brass, and cut in sunder the bars of iron."

Brenda had used drugs for 25 years, and I had all but given up on her. When she came into the detention center, I was happy that she was there because at least I knew how bad off she was. Although I had the keys, I could not open the door. This saying took on a new meaning later on in my life.

For the thirty days she was in jail awaiting her trial, I looked for programs that would not only help her with her drug addiction, but with employment opportunities as well. As difficult as it was for me to come to work and see my sister in jail, I was determined to stand by her and fight for her to be delivered from that horrible addiction. I have seen the effects of addiction, and I know what people do to satisfy their habits. There were women in jail on drug charges who did some unspeakable things just to get another hit. I grabbed hold of my sister and purposed that I would help her to beat this addiction because I refused to leave her in jail.

On three separate occasions, I had to bail her out of jail because she had warrants for her arrest. Her past had finally caught up with her. While she was in the program, I attended every group she had so I could understand her addiction and how I could better help her. Although the program was a one year program, she stayed for two years because it helped her to deal with some unresolved issues.

Brenda eventually had to come to terms with her addiction, confront the cause

of her addiction and learn how to deal with
the stresses of life without seeking solace in
drugs. Needless to say, this did not happen
overnight. The process took a number of
years. She had a relapse once, but eventually,
she managed to beat her addiction. She is
now assisting women who are still battling
addiction through a program she started
called WRAPP (Women Recovering and
Proudly Praising). I am so proud of her and
she knows that I will do whatever I can to
assist her in ensuring her success. By helping
her, I found my purpose in life because I now
have passion and compassion for hurting
women.

In 2006, I was transferred to the
Maryland Correctional Institution for
Women in Jessup. After I got settled in, I
began reaching out to help the women there
(emotionally, not financially), by developing
programs that would help build their self-

esteem, encouraging and motivating them to be and do better. It was there that I had the vision for a transitional house for women who had been released from incarceration, called *Winning the War Within Restoration House.*

Currently, I'm still looking for the money to open the house. It is a two-year program that will focus on education, job placement, and eventually, permanent housing.

I know that a lot of what we as women deal with is a result of low self-esteem, causing us to accept whatever is handed to us. It doesn't matter what our social-economic status in life is, we all struggle with self-esteem issues.

Working at the women's prison gave me the opportunity to meet some women who I had a lot in common with. The only difference between them and me was just that they got caught for their crimes, but through the mercy of God, I did not. My crimes may not have been murder (but could have been), drugs, prostitution or theft, but what I will say is that had I gotten caught, or if I had acted out my plan to kill Russell, I would have been where they are.

It was when I found that I was able to relate to some of those women that I began to acknowledge, confront and deal with my own issues. Needless to say, we all have the potential to commit any or all of those crimes, given the right circumstances.

While working at the women's prison, I was assigned to be the Programs' Activities Supervisor and I was asked to develop some programs to help the women. The first issue I wanted to address was the division among the women. I wanted them to stop focusing on their differences and what they didn't like about one another. My goal was to get them to focus on their similarities and come up with ways that they could help each other to grow as individuals. I developed a mentoring program called "Sister-2-Sister." The program was designed to pair the more mature women with the younger women and first-time offenders in order to help them adjust to prison life without violating institutional rules. We paired older women serving life sentences with younger women coming in with life sentences, and we also tried to pair women with similar crimes. We had monthly meetings and a weekly mentoring session. We also developed a form for tracking the violations of every one of the participants. When I retired in 2009, we had 53 mentors and 179 mentees in the program. Another program that was implemented was a college degree program offered through

Anne Arundel Community College, with the help of the warden (Brenda Shell) and the league of women judges who got all of this approved (along with various other programs).

In 2008, National Geographic did a documentary on (MCIW) called *Lockdown: Maryland's Most Dangerous Women*. This highlighted the work that I did with the women in prison. It can still be seen on YouTube.

Encouraging and motivating women to do better was a priority for me because some of the prisoners had accepted that incarceration was their fate in life, not understanding that they had the power to change their future by the choices they made. Sometimes, the hardest person to be honest about is ourselves because we don't like what we see in the mirror. I am still an advocate for pushing women to be all they can be by encouraging them to do introspections. When we face the demons of our past, we can begin to heal from the hurt associated with it. As I began to help the women to understand and confront their pain, they began to see that we were not different; we were only on opposite sides of the door. The reason I could relate better to the women in prison was because I'd spent so many years in church still bound by my past. I was bound because church people made it taboo to address certain issues, and the irony is, I've been a devout Christian since 1994.

The prayer lines were the front lines of deliverance and in many cases, they weren't working because many of us were still covering up our issues and bound by our past. So, after years of being in church while engaging in some destructive behaviors, I was ashamed to tell people what was really going on in my life because the church culture seemed to have done more to further my hurt than help. I often wondered if I was the only one in the church who was struggling.

Being judged harshly and criticized made me not want to reach to out anyone. I soon learned that the people I reached out to were just as hurt and messed up as I was, so they really couldn't help me nor did they have the right to judge me.

For too long, the church made me feel as if I was the only one not living right because most people covered up their sins, and nobody wanted to be honest about their struggles.

When pastors, preachers and church leaders help people understand that we are all fallible beings and none of us have arrived at perfection, we will be in a better position to really help people heal from past hurts and the spirit of self-righteousness will stop taking over our churches. I'm not saying the church as a whole is responsible, but when people are hurt in church, the whole church is blamed.

Heyward did more to help me to understand and deal with my past hurts than the church did. Even though I did not see it at that time, I later realized that he was only trying to help me. With him, I was like a lioness with a thorn stuck in her paw; I was in great pain, and the person who reached out to help remove the thorn was viciously attacked, but through it all, he remained consistent and stable (that's what I needed more than anything). He would tell me, "I see something in you that you don't see in yourself." I really began to understand why

God did not want me to leave him. I realized that so much of what I was trying to hold on to was destroying my chances of true happiness.

No one knew my internal struggles because to the people who knew me, I seemed to have it all together. I was this awesome prayer warrior, a motivator, a preacher/teacher and an all-out good spiritual leader in the church. I was hiding behind the mask of hypocrisy and on the opposite side of my spiritual door.

I became angry at who I had become; it was time to stop shouting and dancing over my issues and begin to deal with me. It was only when I decided to be honest with myself and cry out to God for a real change that I could admit that I was broken both emotionally and spiritually. It was only after I was honest with Got that I was healed, both emotionally and spiritually. I could not help anyone else. I made it my primary goal to confess to God (although He knew what my struggles were), that I needed to be healed from all past hurts and then, allow Him to take me through my process of confronting the real "me" and not the "me" I showed everyone else. I needed to confront the "me" behind closed doors, the "me" I was in my car and the "me" I was with my husband. I had to get away from the emotionalism of church. No longer could I get behind the pulpit to preach, not live what I was preaching and be comfortable with who I was. Heyward helped me to see that what I thought was my personality was, in fact, anger that I had been holding on to.

I had built up a wall of mistrust in order to protect myself from being hurt and just as I wouldn't allow anyone in, I did not let myself out. What Russell tried to do to me physically, I did to myself emotionally, and I had locked myself in my prison of fear and mistrust. Although I had the key, I could not open the door.

Psalm 107:20 Authorized (King James) Version (AKJV)

"He sent his word, and healed them, and delivered them from their destructions."

Even though I've come a long way, I still feel that I have a long way to go.

In 2013, by the leading of the Holy Spirit, I stepped out to pastor my own church. The church is named "Winning the War Within Ministries." I believe that we need to be healed from the inside out. No more trying to cover up our flaws, inadequacies, insecurities and self-righteous attitudes. When we understand that we are no better or no different than the next person, regardless of our economic or social status, it will be easier to embrace and help each other.

Nowadays, I no longer see myself as a savior, but as a sister who is in the process of healing from her past so that she can help others through their process. I have the courage and strength to be honest enough about who I am, where I am, where I'm trying to go and what I need to get there.

Change is a lifelong process and if we accept and embrace this, we can allow change in every stage of our lives. My prayer is that I can make a significant contribution by impacting the lives of the women I meet in my life's journey. The words my husband spoke to me, "I see something in you that you don't see in yourself," are the words I can now say to another woman because I have learned to look past what is apparent and look at what is potential, not only in others, but in myself as well.

When I opened myself and let the healing begin, it was easier to see that I've always had the keys to open my prison door. I am now able to walk out of my prison of hurt, distrust, anger, unforgiveness, insecurity and needing to do it all myself by allowing others in to help.

I've learned that I can say I don't have all the answers, I can't save everybody, and I will fail from time to time, but that's okay. I'm not assigned to help everyone, but I am assigned to help someone. I am still where I need to be while I am on my journey to where I'm going. "I'm free."

BRENDA'S STORY

I was the fourth of seven children and I discovered a way to manipulate my mother when I was a child. I knew that if I cried before my punishment, she would be lenient on me. This type of behavior followed me even to this day. Shedding tears is very easy for me to do and it has always had a way of causing people to sympathize with me. My life took a devastating turn after the death of my son. Yes, I did experiment with marijuana as a teenager, but it wasn't until Jason's death and having my daughter taken from me and placed in the care of my mother, that my downward spiral with drugs really began. My then live-in-boyfriend, Tyrone, was incarcerated for killing my son. I was in night school, trying to get my GED when two police officers came and got me out of class. They told me that some officers had caught Tyrone holding Jason by the back of his neck. He was just about to throw him over the wall across from where we lived when the officers caught him. They said I needed to go to with them to the University of Maryland Hospital.

When we arrived at the hospital, I was escorted to the emergency department and told that Jason had expired. Seeing my baby lying on the bed lifeless was too much for me to bear. I wanted answers, but I didn't get any. I kept asking myself why Tyrone would take my son's life.

We later found out that he had physically abused my daughter by beating her and he'd broken her hipbone. I blamed myself because I left my children with a man who did harm to them and I did not know what was going on. He was not just any man, I met him in church and I thought I could trust him. I tried to go on with my life, but it was just too hard. My son was dead and my daughter was taken away from me and placed in the care of my mother. At that moment, I didn't want to hear anything about God. There was absolutely nothing anyone could say to convince me that God existed and there was nothing anyone could say to encourage me. I turned my back on God, but He never turned his back on me. I was angry and I did not know what to do. I was an emotional mess and I needed something or someone to help me to cope.

I later started dating a guy by the name of Jeff. He was the brother of a friend of mine and he was in the military. I moved to North Carolina where Jeff lived, and we got married. It was there that I was introduced to cocaine and I found that the drug seemed to help me to cope with my pain. Of course, that "help" was short-lived and Jeff soon became verbally and physically abusive towards me. To cope with his abuse, I started using more.

I stayed with Jeff for three years before I was finally tired of his abusive ways. After I left him, I came back to Baltimore to live with my mother and daughter. I eventually regained custody of my daughter, but by this time, I had been using drugs regularly. Nevertheless, I was able to hide my heavy usage from my family. Jeff had gotten out of the military and moved back to Baltimore with his mother and we ended up reconciling our relationship. My daughter really liked Jeff, but the abuse continued, so I sent her to live with my mother again. By this time, I was not only using marijuana and cocaine, but I had started "popping" pills. Jeff blamed me for his inability to find work, so the abuse got worse. At one point, he almost killed me. Again, I left him, but this time, I did not go back. We finally got divorced, and not only was I not healed from the pain of losing my son, but I went through this abusive relationship for five years only to find myself alone and with a drug addiction.

I soon met another man named Eugene and we started living together, but again, the physical abuse and the drug use continued. I didn't realize that my life had spun out of control and that I was always trying to ease my pain by looking for drugs and someone who would support my habit.

After two years of abuse, I left him and moved back in with my mother. She was finally tired of me living with her, so she helped me find my own place. She thought she was helping me, but she wasn't. She even paid the first month's rent and security deposit, but because of my addiction, I was unable to keep the place because all of my money went towards drugs.

I soon lost my apartment and had to move in with my mother again; she just could not turn her back on me. Once again, I met another man (Tony) and the drug use continued. Although my family knew that I was addicted to drugs, they did not know what drugs I was addicted to.

I was eventually introduced to heroin and it became my drug of choice. Heroin was my lover, my husband, my mother, my daughter and my comforter. Anything I needed it to be, that's what it was. I developed this pattern of getting involved with men who abused me, but as long as they were able to supply me with the drugs, I tolerated their abuse. I eventually got my own place in a high rise building on Orleans

Street and my daughter came to live with me, but because of the drug use and abusive relationships I kept getting into, she eventually lost all respect for me. After she was old enough to leave, she wanted nothing else to do with me. I knew she loved me, but she could no longer deal with my lifestyle. I finally left Tony, but by then, my drug addiction had totally consumed me. I did whatever I had to do to get high. I went from stealing to prostitution, stripping and doing whatever was required of me to feed my addiction, and this is how I met my second husband, Ed. I convinced him to let me move in with him and we were married shortly thereafter.

He was a recovering alcoholic himself and a bit naïve. He unknowingly became my enabler because he was willing to get me the drugs in order to keep me off the streets. There is a possibility that he did know that he was an enabler because of his own addiction, but manipulating him was easy. At that time, I was truly in need of the drugs because I had become a slave to them. I would do any and everything for a fix, but of course, that's what drugs do to people. Even though Ed was an enabler, he didn't allow my addiction to take him back down the path of his addiction. He was a truck driver, and when he was away, my demand outweighed his supply so I started making deposits into the ATM machine using an empty envelope. I had discovered that I could withdraw one hundred dollars off of a deposit using this method. I would withdraw the money and get more drugs. When I could no longer steal from the bank (because Ed was forced to close the account), I began calling him while he was at work and making him come home to buy drugs for me. Because of my addiction, Ed lost several jobs trying to keep me happy.

Brenda's Story

After losing our home, we moved in with my daughter in Curtis Bay. Gee Gee loved Ed like a father and he is the only grandfather that my granddaughters know to this day. We were moving from place to place because that is where my addiction took us.

Ed loved me so much that he would follow me everywhere I went. It didn't matter how low I went, he was right there with me. It had gotten so bad that I would leave Ed in whatever house we were staying in and I would walk around outside late at night with crack in one hand and heroin in the other. I would find a dark place to get high, not even thinking about how dangerous it was and that anything could happen to me while I was out there. It is common for women on the street to get raped and robbed. As soon as my high came down, I would go back to prostituting to get more. I now know that God's hand of protection was on me, even when I was in my mess. Ed would patiently wait for me to come back to him and even put up with my mistreatment of him.

We were married for ten years, and this time, I became the abuser. That's how I ended up in jail. I assaulted Ed for the last time when I violently struck him across his head with a skillet and injured him. It was then that his mother called the police on me. I was arrested and taken to Central Booking where I was booked and charged. When I could not make bail, I was sent to Baltimore City Jail, Women's Detention Center.

I had no idea that my sister worked there. I knew that she worked in the Division of Corrections, and the last prison I remembered her working in was the Maryland State Penitentiary, so my arrest was just an arrest to me. I did not know that it was the beginning of my recovery.

When I saw Debbora, I was shocked, but glad because I knew that I would be alright. The next day, a church group came in to minister to the women and my brother, Charles, was a part of that group. I knew God was involved in these events because I was in a jail where my sister worked, and to have my brother's church group (the church that I grew up in), come in and minister was not just coincidental, it was destiny.

While in jail, I went through drug withdrawal and it was horrible. I was sick most of the time, and there were many times when I could not get out of bed, but because of the routine of the jail, I was forced to get involved in some of the activities. The prison was not equipped to deal with addicts going through withdrawal, so I had to go through my withdrawal without any help.

Because Debbora was a sergeant and the officers had a lot of respect for her, they looked out for me, making sure I was not attacked by any of the other inmates. There were even some officers who talked to me about the Lord and encouraged me.

I did not get to see much of Debbora while she was at work because she had other responsibilities, but she did come to check on me at least once a night. I did not understand that this was her job and she had to treat me like every other prisoner, and because of this, there were times that I felt that she deserted me.

Debbora found a drug treatment program to get me into and she bailed me out of jail. I was glad to be free.

The judge dropped my assault charge when I went to court, but to my surprise, when I was leaving the courtroom, a sheriff deputy came up behind me and said, "Come with me." As it turned out, there was another warrant out for my arrest. My past was catching up with me. I was again taken over to the Women's Detention Center, where I had to remain until my next court date. This time, Debbora wrote the judge a letter, explaining to the judge who she was, who I was and how she intended to help me. She asked the judge to remand me to the drug treatment program she had gotten me into.

The judge said that after reading her letter, he knew from his years of experience that when people have the support of their family, recovery is almost always successful, so he stipulated that I go to the program.

I then found out that I had another warrant out for my arrest under an alias, and this time, Debbora came and took me to Central Booking to be booked and charged with the promise of bailing me out. All of my past had to be dealt with in order for me to get a fresh start in life. She kept true to her word and I received my bail. After I was escorted to the receiving area to be processed for my release, I felt that it was finally over.

While I was being escorted through the tunnel from the Women's Detention Center to go through to Central Booking Intake, the officer stopped me and said they could not let me go. I thought I had done something wrong, but the officer said that my sister, Sergeant Hanna, told them to hold me there until she got off from work. If she did not stop me, it is very likely that I would have been back on the streets in a situation that I did not need to be in. When she got off, she took me back to the drug treatment program.

I don't know what I would have done if she had not been there for me; she was and still is my angel. God saw it fit to put her in a place to help me at a time I thought I would die in my addiction, but He had better plans for me.

The drug treatment program was a starting point for me to stay clean, and they did what they could, even though I did not agree with some of their methods. My withdrawals continued while I was in the program. I spent many days in and out of the emergency room because I was always sick from the withdrawals.

The doctors were surprised that I used drugs for as long as I did because I did not have the effects of long-term drug abuse. I didn't shoot heroin; I snorted it. It was nothing but the favor of God that it did not damage my nasal passage, nor did I contract any sexually transmitted diseases from my days of prostituting.

The program did not offer any real counseling, which was something I really needed, but I thank God that I survived. It helped me to get hired by Denise Marketing. I was sure that my life had finally taken a turn for the better.

After I completed two years of the program, I thought that I was okay. I thought I could make it on my own, only to find out that I was not as strong as I thought I was, so I relapsed.

I am thankful to God that although I relapsed, I did not stay on drugs for too long

because I did not want to go back to that
lifestyle. I was really afraid that if I did not
come back from that relapse, I would
definitely die in my addiction. I've learned
that I can never say what I won't do because
sometimes, our circumstances make
decisions for us. I was afraid to tell Debbora,
especially after she had done so much for me,
so I tried to go at it alone.

My third husband, Kevin, whom I met
in the program, stood by me. He did not
know what to do about my drug use, so he
would always go with me when I went to
purchase drugs because he wanted to ensure
my safety. I made him promise me that he
would not tell my family about my relapse, so
we ended up homeless. We ended up living
under the Falls Way Bridge and going from
shelter to shelter.

I did not have to be homeless. I could have moved in with my daughter, but she would not let Kevin move in, so I chose to stay homeless with him.

We would go to Code Blue in the evening. Code Blue was a homeless shelter across from the courthouse on Saratoga Street. We had to be there by 3:30 every afternoon to get a bed, and we had to be out with all our things by seven o'clock every morning. By then, my family knew that I had relapsed and they still stuck by and supported me.

We spent four months in a shelter and our counselor helped us to get an apartment through their program. I was referred to a Health Care Services establishment called Chase Brexton, and it was there that I received counseling services, health care services and a lot of support.

I overcame my addiction and am still very much involved with Chase Brexton, where I attend and hold weekly WRAPP sessions. I now live my life for Jesus Christ because it was He who changed my life and ordered my steps.

My daughter, who wanted nothing to do with me in my addiction, is thrilled about my recovery. I also have two beautiful granddaughters who I am very proud of: Breonica is sixteen and Nyesha is ten. I am married to a wonderful man (Kevin), who is very supportive of me and the work I do in ministry. My sister, Debbora, is my pastor and I am on the praise and worship team at her church. I only see a bright future ahead for me, and now, I only surround myself with people who will encourage me to do and be better. It is now my turn to give back and I do this through a group that I started called

(WRAPP) Women Recovering and Proudly Praising.

I know what it is like to have an addiction, so I want to help as many women as I can to overcome their addictions and begin a new life. When I think about all of the years of my life that were lost to drugs and how much more I could have accomplished, I am inspired to fight with everything in me to help others the same way my sister and others fought for me.

OUR STORY

Although our story may not be typical, I believe almost every woman can find some of herself in what we've gone through, whether physical, emotional or spiritual.

Prison is not just steel bars and metal beds, it's a mindset. We can be behind bars yet be free in our minds and not be limited by our circumstances.

We have the keys to be free, yet we refuse to open the doors that are holding us captive. There is nothing holding us back except us. Growing up, my mother taught my siblings and me to love one another. I believe she was passionate about this because she so desperately wanted it for herself; she made sure that we stuck together even through the hard times.

What I found to be so amazing about our story was that, as teenagers, Brenda and I never really got along. We fought like strangers and it was hard for me to be in the same room with her for more than 30 minutes without an argument ensuing. Many times, my mother and my sister, Barbara, would have to intervene and break up our fights. As we got older, we spent less time around each other because our lives were going in different directions. Little did we know that the time we spent apart was the time God used to order our steps and get us to where we are today. As a pastor, God had to develop in me compassion for not just hurting women, but hurting people. Corrections had made me a little cynical and

I could not treat the people of God like inmates. I had to change my approach in how I dealt with people because I needed to be less authoritative and more compassionate. Ministry is more than just preaching a word, but touching the core of an individual so they will have the courage to face who they really are and be healed from within.

I used to tell my mother that she birthed Brenda in the natural, but God used me to birth her in the spirit through prayer. Brenda now does praise and worship at the church and God has really anointed her to sing, but God is preparing her for so much more.

God has called us to labor in the spirit for the lives of our unsaved loved ones. We can't continue to try and save the world when our families are dying right in front of us. Yes, sometimes it's harder with family because they remember who we were, how we used to be, and many times, they'll remind us of what we did in our pasts. Nevertheless, unbeknownst to them, God used all of that time to order our steps to get us to where we are now.

John 1:7 Authorized (King James) Version (AKJV)

"The same came for a witness, to bear witness of the Light that all men through him might believe."

Philippians 3:13 Authorized (King James) Version (AKJV)

"Brethren, I count not myself to have apprehended: but this one thing I do, forgetting those things which are behind, and reaching forth unto those things which are before."

I have learned to let go of my past, failures, disappointments, mistakes and intentional screw-ups because they don't define me. I can't change what was; I can only focus on what is and what will be.

Growing up for me, happened too quickly because I thrust myself into adulthood. I wanted to get out of my mother's house, not fully comprehending the emotional responsibility that came with adulthood and the complexity of making adult decisions.

Life was not always easy, but there were many lessons I learned in life that have drastically changed me for the better.

What I thought was weakness in my mother, I now see as strength. She'd endured all she went through and still managed to keep our family together in spite of her personal failures and lack of resources. She did the best that she knew how to do with the hand that life dealt her.

We all have a path in life that we must follow and we all have our own crosses to bear. My mother is my biggest supporter and cheerleader in my life's journey. I appreciate the woman who raised me and my siblings. I am in the family God placed me in, and for that, I'm grateful.

I am now continuing down the path that God is taking me. I'm still reaching out to hurting people, but now I do it through a program offered by the city of Baltimore. In addition to pastoring, I am now working with the Lead Hazard Reduction Program. Through this program, we reach out to homeowners with potential lead paint in their homes, and through a grant funded program, we make their homes lead safe for the benefit of their children. In this position,

I've met some amazing women and one of them is a woman named Faith. My initial encounter with Faith was to talk about the transitional home I'm trying to open. I had been referred to her by a friend of mine, but after speaking with her and listening to her life's experience, I thought she would be a great addition to the book so she agreed to share her story.

FAITH'S STORY

I was the first of three children born to my parents. They were excited to have a newborn baby because, at the age of twenty-eight, my mother was afraid that she couldn't have children, but God had other plans. Being the first child and the first girl born into my family, my father spoiled me terribly. I was definitely daddy's little girl. One hot summer day, I remember my father coming to the house in his work truck. He worked for a furniture company. As he was pulling in, I saw the ice cream man.

I asked my dad for a Dream Cycle ice cream and he brought it for me. I sat in his truck and ate the ice cream, thinking to myself that it was the best ice cream I'd ever had. That was the last thing I remembered about my father. I don't remember seeing him anymore after that, neither do I remember seeing my mother anymore because she was gone for a while as well. As a child, the adults didn't discuss "grown folks" business with children. I guess that's the difference between the adults then and the adults now; we knew our place.

One day, a friend of my mother came and got my brother and I. She said that we were going to stay with her. I didn't know where my parents were, and as the time passed, my brother and I apparently forgot our parents because we stopped asking for them. One day, a woman appeared and asked my brother and I if we remembered her. My brother looked at her and shook his head, indicating that he didn't remember who she was. I looked at my brother and said, "I think that is Mom." She smiled and responded with, "Yes, it is me." My mother had been incarcerated the entire time for the murder of my father. Of course, we had many unanswered questions about what happened to him and how he died.

She served a short time in prison because all of the charges were eventually dropped and she was released, nevertheless, I was still upset with her because I did not know all the details surrounding my father's death. I did not know that she had killed him while defending herself from his abuse. In my mind, she'd murdered my father and that was the end of the story. My mother worked hard to care for her children. She even cleaned other people's homes to make ends meet. My uncle would come to our home every morning to care for us when she left for work.

One day, I asked my mother not to leave us with my uncle, but she told me that she had to work. What she didn't know was that every day when he came to care for us, he would send my brother and sister outside to play. After they went outside, he would take me into the bathroom and molest me. I was so afraid to tell my mother, but I knew I couldn't keep that secret for too long. One day, I finally built up the courage to tell my mother what her brother was doing to me, and she was livid. She immediately asked him to leave our house. Before leaving, he asked if he could use the bathroom, and after he left, my mother went into the bathroom and saw the horror scene that he left behind. He'd placed his feces all over the walls and on the bath towels. Of course, we never saw him again. I believe that incident played a very important role in my relationships with men.

I struggled with the death of my father, while blaming my mother. Plus, I didn't fully understand how to deal with or process what my uncle had done to me, so I began to make some really bad decisions. I desperately wanted someone to notice and love me. Growing up in the sixties with very dark skin was difficult. I learned that the lighter complexioned females got most of the attention. They were more popular, seemed to get picked for the better jobs and they definitely stood out with the young guys. That's when I began to develop low self-esteem. We moved into public housing where I was finally approached by a guy who was interested in me. I was excited to finally have a boyfriend. I soon learned that my new boyfriend was abusive, but I thought his behavior was normal. After all, when I was a child, I had watched my father abuse my mother many times. I thought hitting me was his way of showing love, so I accepted his behavior as normal. My relationship became more and more volatile, so my mother told me to end the relationship because of what she'd gone through with my father. She did not want the same thing to happen to me. My ex-boyfriend eventually joined the Job Corps and he went out of my life temporarily.

While walking down the street one summer day, my friend saw a beautiful yellow Cutlass Oldsmobile heading our way. As it turned out, the owner and I had attended High School together. We ended up having a brief relationship and I got pregnant. Most of the young girls in public housing had babies, but I'd planned to be different. I did not want to become a statistic, but unfortunately, I did.

My mother made the decision to move from public housing and we ended up purchasing a home. We moved to a fairly decent neighborhood and I gave birth to my little girl the following month. For a couple of years, I struggled with trying to work and take care of my daughter. During this time, the young man who abused me came home for a visit from the Job Corps. He thought my daughter was his daughter, so he wanted to restart our relationship. We rekindled our relationship, but the abuse continued.

One day, he called and asked me if he could purchase some clothes for my daughter for the upcoming holiday. I said yes. We decided to meet the next day, and while I was getting dressed to meet him, I received a call from one of my friends. She told me that the man I was getting dressed to go and meet had been killed the night before. I was devastated, but that was the life he chose to live.

One night, I went to a local club and that's where I met a wonderful sailor. We dated for about two years, and after that, we decided to get married. Once he left the Navy, he started working at General Motors, while I worked as a personnel administrator for a finance company. We both had great salaries and the only thing that was bad in our marriage was the fact that we worked different shifts. He worked the night shift and I worked days. On several occasions, I suggested that he change his shift, but he didn't want to lose the difference in pay, so he continued to work nights. I was fired from the finance company so I went to work for a hospital.

One day, I ran into an old friend from public housing at work and we decided to have lunch together. He was at the hospital because his wife was in labor. This meeting turned out to change the course of my life for the worse. I had no idea that he was a drug dealer and that this chanced meeting would take me down a path of destruction. Even though I had previously indulged in drugs for pleasure, I had never engaged in heavy drugs. I felt alone at night because my husband was never home, but of course, this does not justify my actions. I was young and had my whole life ahead of me. I felt that I was wasting my life on someone who did not appreciate me. Larry (the drug-dealer friend of mine) showered me with everything I wanted, including heroin. We began to see each other every day and we pretty much spent almost every night together. To us, it didn't matter that we were married. Needless to say, both marriages ended in separations, and for me, my marriage ultimately ended in a divorce. Larry's wife had a nervous breakdown because of our affair. Yes, I was being selfish; I was only thinking about my own happiness, but little did I know that happiness was not in my future with him.

Larry and I started living together and I began using drugs heavily. I stayed up all night doing drugs, and amazingly enough, I was still able to report to work on time every day. Because of this, I thought that I could handle my drug usage. Eventually, I lost my job and my place, so we ended up homeless. My sister and mother took my daughter, and from there, my life continued to spiral out of control.

We lived in homes that had no electricity, plus, we didn't have food or money for our basic necessities, but we always managed to find money for drugs.

Eventually, I found a job and got a house, and from there, my daughter and his two children came to live with us.

We tried to live a normal life as a
family, but the drugs made it virtually
impossible to be normal. We couldn't even
make sure the kids were kept on track. I
went to work every day under the influence
of drugs, and Larry stayed home selling
them. His youngest daughter failed
kindergarten because he couldn't get up
early enough to send her to school.

Larry's addiction was so bad that
when he smoked crack, he would hear voices
and start hallucinating. Every night, his
brother and his brother's girlfriend would
come over to our house to smoke crack. Since
I was the only one in the house who worked,
I would go to bed early and they would stay
in the living room smoking crack.

During his hallucinations, Larry would
come into the bedroom and ask me if I'd
heard anything, and I would tell him that I

hadn't. One of his most frequent hallucinations was of me talking to a man outside the window and this went on for months. He then started to accuse me of having an affair because of the man he thought he saw outside of my window. One night, he came home and asked me for his drugs. I didn't know where the drugs were, but he didn't believe me so he accused me of lying. He then took a belt and beat me over the head with the belt's buckle. Blood was everywhere.

As I tried to leave, he continued to beat me until I was able to get out of the house. I managed to run to a neighbor's house and call my mother. She told me to call a taxi and come over to her house. What I found out about domestic violence is that once an abuser starts to beat on his/ her victim, the abuse never stops. It's a cycle of violence that never ends.

Because I was a heroin addict, I thought I had no other choice but to deal with it, so the beatings continued and I continued to endure them. I would go to work with black eyes. Of course, I would try to cover it up with make-up, but that didn't work very well. Every payday, Larry would come to my job to get my check. I didn't have control over my money. One payday, I had just cashed my check and Larry and I were on our way to the hospital to see my mother. He told me to give him my check, but by that time, I was truly fed up with his abuse so I refused to give it to him. He then took his fist and punched me across my right eye. The impact was so bad that I thought I saw stars and all of my money flew out of the car's window. I was very upset. I pulled the car over, jumped out of it and picked up as much of my money as I could find. Once I arrived at the hospital, my mother looked up and asked me what had happened to my face, and of course, I said that nothing had happened. She said to me that all the makeup in the world wouldn't cover up the black eye I'd just received. This was a wake up call for me, and after a long struggle with my addiction and putting up with Larry's abuse, I finally had enough. I began to plan my exit from him, so each day when I went to work, I would remove some of my belongings. Once everything was out of the house, I called him to tell him that I would not be returning. He asked me the silliest question: "What about your clothes?" I told him that if he checked the closet, he would see that they weren't there. I was finally free from that toxic relationship.

My sister had an apartment and I decided to take my daughter and move in with her. I realized that I needed help with my addiction, so I entered a drug treatment program because I could not kick the habit on my own. I got on the methadone program because I could not handle the symptoms of withdrawal and I found that it worked better for me.

When I started the program, I decided to not be in it for any more than four years and I told myself that I would not become familiar with the clients involved. There is a culture within the methadone community because unfortunately, methadone draws people to crack cocaine, so most people are not really beating their addiction, they're just replacing it with another one. I ended up having another addiction, and this time, it was to crack cocaine. I began using methadone and crack cocaine interchangeably. Eventually, my rent was in arrears and my bills were not being paid. I was headed back down the same path of destruction. Larry wanted to come back into my life because he was homeless, so I told him that he could stay at my place during the night because I worked the day shift. He agreed with the arrangements and moved back in with me.

One night, Larry did not come home before my scheduled bedtime, so I locked the door. When I woke up the next morning, I was surprised to see that he still had not come home, nevertheless, I went to work. While at work, I happened to look up at the entrance and saw two people talking to my supervisor. She led them to my desk and said to me that the two detectives wanted to speak with me. They asked me if I knew Larry Jones and I said that I did. They then asked me if I would come with them to the morgue. My heart was racing and I felt like I was having an out of body experience. Once we arrived at the morgue, the detectives told me to have a seat and then, they rolled Larry's body out on a table for me to identify.

Just seeing the bullet holes in his ear and head was traumatizing for me and the detectives asked me questions that I had no answers for. It turned out that Larry had taken money from the people he was selling drugs for and when they caught up with him, they killed him. I suddenly realized that I had to change my life or Larry's fate would also be mine. My family feared that whoever was responsible for Larry's death would come looking for me because Larry had taken these drug dealers money and could not pay them back. That's when I made the decision to change my life. I asked God to show me the way out of the lifestyle and He did.

Not long after I decided to stop using drugs, my mother was diagnosed with colon cancer, so I decided to move in with her to take care of her. That's when she finally told me the story surrounding my father's death. My mother told me that while she was at work, my father would have women at their house. One day, she came home and caught him in bed with another woman. To her surprise, my father began to beat her and that's when she called the police. While she was talking to the 911 operator, my father ran outside with my mother in pursuit of him. She always carried a pocket knife and she said that when she caught up with him, they argued, she pulled out the pocket knife and lunged towards my father, sticking him in his chest. My father fell to the ground and my mother kept telling him to get up. Finally, she helped him up and took him to the University of Maryland Hospital, which was not far away. When they arrived at the hospital, my father was taken to the back for treatment and the police came and spoke with my mother. She said that the police asked for her version of the incident because, according to the arresting officers, my father had already told them his version. She explained the events of that fateful night to them, and then, she asked if she could see him but they told her that he was deceased and she was arrested.

I finally got to hear the story from my mother's perspective; she died one year later. I am so thankful that I was able to bond with and forgive my mother before she passed.

I started surrounding myself with positive people who were doing positive things. I attended church, even though I was still on a methadone program and working. I began to detoxify myself off the methadone and worked towards mending my relationships with the people I hurt when I was a slave to the drugs. I completed the methadone program within three years and detoxed myself because I was determined not to give drugs another day to ruin my life or another chance to take my life. You never know how God plans to use you to help someone else. After I got my degree and became an addictions counselor, my plan was to focus on my recovery. God again had other plans and I was offered a position as a coordinator of a recovery center working with women who were addicts. That was a very rewarding time in my life because I felt that I was giving back. After working at that facility for five years, I was diagnosed with lung cancer. I decided at that time that it was time for me to give up counseling and focus on my health.

I started smoking cigarettes at the age of sixteen and I was smoking at least two packs a day.

As I got older, I always kept my appointments for mammograms and my doctor always insisted that I get a chest x-ray along with my mammograms. In June 2002, I had my mammogram and chest x-rays done. I received a letter from the radiology facility stating that everything was fine with the mammogram, but the radiology report showed that there was a spot on my lung. When I heard the news, my heart dropped and I started planning my funeral because to me that was a death sentence.

The doctor sent me to see a specialist and the specialist reviewed my chest x-rays and said that I was definitely going to die, but not from this. He immediately scheduled me for surgery. I had the surgery and they removed the left lobe of my lung. I was in intensive care for two days and then they transferred me to a surgical unit where I stayed for another day. My total time in the hospital was three days. I was determined to not allow the surgery to get me down. I was discharged from the hospital and went home.

My sister came from South Carolina to help me and my recovery went well. It has been thirteen years now, and to God be the glory, I am still going strong.

After my recovery from drugs was improving and the cancer was in remission, I felt compelled to help women who were in abusive relationships and caught up in drug addiction. I wanted to help them to see that with the help of God, their lives could be better if they worked at it. The response was overwhelming because several women from the recovery center needed some place to stay.

One day, a young lady who had applied for a job, came into my office for an interview. We talked and she indicated that she was interested in opening a transitional house for women so, instead of her working for me, we got together, asked for donations for furniture and we located a house. Within three months, we opened a transitional house and housed six women. That was seven years ago and she is still running the house to this day.

Although my life improved considerably and I was successful in my career, unfortunately, my past caught up with me. Earlier I mentioned that I was fired from the financial company that I worked for and in 1979. A few of my coworkers and I had embezzled some checks from that company. I embezzled over fifty thousand dollars, but I'm not sure how much my co-workers took. When we went to court, we were ordered to pay restitution and complete our probation; that would have ended it, but I didn't pay my restitution like the other women did. When people say your past will come to haunt you, they are telling the truth.

It was in 2014 that my past caught up with me. I was at work one day and I went out to move my car because I was parked in a four hour parking space. All of a sudden, an unmarked police car blocked me in and the officer driving the car asked me for my name. When I told him, he said to me that there was a warrant out for my arrest. I was definitely caught off guard and couldn't believe what was happening to me. I couldn't tell my supervisor that I was being arrested because I was not allowed to go back to my office. I asked the officer if I could call my daughter to come and get my car because I did not want it impounded and he agreed. I was taken to Central Booking and denied bail because I was a direct intake. The only way that I was going to see a judge was to have an attorney get a motion for me to see one. I had to pay an attorney fifteen hundred dollars to get that motion.

The judge was unmerciful. She said the only way I was getting out of jail was if I paid the ten thousand dollar cash bond.

My daughter went to get ten money orders in the amount of one thousand dollars each, and then, we went before the judge. Even though the parole and probation officers were satisfied with the restitution, the judge was not. She wanted the money to come out of my personal account. I explained to the judge that I had paid my daughter back, but she still was not satisfied, even though she could not hold me because I had satisfied my obligation. I understand that what I did was wrong and I should pay for my crime, but the judge treated me like I had killed somebody. No one wants to be an addict and that definitely wasn't a part of my plan for life. Even though I spent years trying to get my life back on track, was drug free, got a degree and had a successful career, my past was all that mattered to the judge. She was determined to put me away, but I am thankful to God that He had another plan for my life. A nun at the correctional center told me that God had a plan for me and that is why I was there.

In the short time that I was in the detention center, I mentored several females. Once I was released, I reached out to some of the ladies that I met there, and to this day, we all have a wonderful relationship with one another. Glory to God, He had me there to reach these ladies. I've put my past behind me and I am very happy with my life the way it is, and with what I was able to accomplish through the grace of God.

UNLOCKING THE PRISON OF OUR MINDS

Any one of our stories could be your story. Unfortunately, we sometimes allow many of life's experiences to polarize us, but they do not have to. I refused to allow another man to get close to me and I almost missed out on the wonderful relationship I now have with Heyward. I know that some of you have gone through a lot worse than what we've gone through, but because you are still here and in your right mind, it is safe to say that God has a plan and purpose for your life.

We keep ourselves imprisoned by many things including the fear of failure, the opinions of others and the limitations of our comfort zones.

Helen, a 64 year old woman, was locked in the prison of her mind for 64 years. She was given up for adoption because her mother did not want her, and she was mistreated by her adoptive parents. For years, Helen was made to feel like she was insignificant, ugly and unwanted. She had very low self-esteem and she allowed people to make her feel bad about herself. When she got married, she gave total control of her life to her husband and allowed him to make all of the decisions for her. For 29 years, she was clueless about any of the household expenses because he did everything. When she asked him questions about the bills, he told her that she did not need to know, so Helen accepted life the way it was because she thought he really loved her.

Helen was diagnosed with pancreatic cancer and she thought she was going to die before her husband, but when he died in March of 2015, Helen was lost. She did not know where anything was or what to do. She relied on others to help her, only to find out that they were taking advantage of her.

Not only did she have to grieve his death, but she had to try to figure out how to take responsibility over her own life, finances and financial responsibilities.

After the counseling Helen received from her pastor, she began to take control of her life. It was hard at times because she still struggled with low self-esteem, but she started to unlock the prison of her mind, taking back and using the keys she had given to others. She is still receiving counseling, but she is stronger now than she was before.

God had different plans for Helen than she had for herself.

We don't have to be perfect. One of the greatest mistakes in life is to try to be someone you're not.

- Give yourself permission to express your feelings.

- Give yourself permission to be angry.

- Give yourself permission to hurt.

- Give yourself permission to grieve over and bury your past, but also give yourself permission to forgive, heal and move on.

We are always on opposite sides of a door because there are many of life's doors that imprison us: doors of abuse, doors of shame and guilt, doors of financial debt, doors of envy and jealousy etc...... we can choose what side we remain on. Whatever your door is you have the keys to unlock it. We have the keys to success, and not utilizing those keys will guarantee our failure.

It's time to come out of the prison of your mind, use the keys you've been given to unlock and unleash your potential and soar into your future. It is never too late unless you're dead.

The lyrics to the song *You are More* by Tenth Avenue North:

There's a girl in the corner with tear stains on her eyes from the places she's wandered and the shame she can't hide.

She says, "How did I get here? I'm not who I once was. And I'm crippled by the fear that I've fallen too far to love"

*But don't you know who you are, what's been
done for you? Yeah, don't you know who you
are?*

*You are more than the choices that you've
made, you are more than the sum of your past
mistakes,*
*you are more than the problems you create,
you've been remade.*

2 Corinthians 5:17 Authorized (King James) Version (AKJV)

*"Therefore if any man be in Christ, he is a new
creature: old things are passed away; behold,
all things are become new."*

**YOU CAN BE FREE!!!!!!!!! YOU CAN BE
REMADE!!!!!!!!!!**

By Debbora Hanna

www.ingramcontent.com/pod-product-compliance
Lightning Source LLC
Chambersburg PA
CBHW060806050426
42449CB00008B/1563